NEVER MIND THE TARTAN ARMY

The Ultimate SCOTTISH FOOTBALL QUIZ BOOK

DAVID POTTER

D1395653

To all those who have followed Scotland for as long
as I have … and suffered just as much.

First published 2015

The History Press
The Mill, Brimscombe Port
Stroud, Gloucestershire, GL5 2QG
www.thehistorypress.co.uk

British Library Cataloguing in Publication Data.
A catalogue record for this book is available from the British Library.

ISBN 978 0 7509 6073 1

Typesetting and origination by The History Press
Printed in Great Britain

Contents

Introduction

You really have no choice about it. If you are Scottish, you really have to support the national team! There are those who feign indifference and even hostility to the performances of the Scotland national side, but their pretence is usually rumbled when they spend half an hour telling you WHY they no longer support the team. The laddies 'doth protest too much', one feels.

It must be owned that recent performances, certainly in the twenty-first century, have not been great. It is ironic that this has happened at a time when life in Scotland in other respects has been buoyant and vibrant, yet in our most popular sport, repeated disappointments to teams like Moldova and Macedonia have been the order of the day. In the meanwhile, sports like cycling and tennis show that there is no reason at all why Scotland cannot be the best in the world.

It was not always like this. Nor does it have to be like this in the future. This book, apart from being fun, is an attempt to remind people of the great days in the past. Not that they were always great days. We had our disasters (repeated ones) at Wembley, the hideous business in Argentina and the 0–7 defeat to Uruguay in 1954, which was your writer's introduction to both Scotland's incompetence and television at the same time. He has been deeply scarred as a result.

But there were also the great days. The 1920s and 1930s saw Scotland more than hold their own against England, and further back, England were repeatedly put to the sword (in the figurative sense of course!) in the 1880s. Great players abounded in Scotland in the years before and after the Great War, and it remains the writer's contention that the World Cup in 1966 could have been won by Scotland instead of England, if only a dire combination of incompetence, underperformance and complacency had not conspired to prevent our qualification.

Players and games from all ages are featured in the nearly 400 questions. Some questions are obvious, others are the province of the footballing geeks, of whom there are an alarming number on occasion. The hope is, however, that interest can be stimulated in Scotland's past, and that enthusiasm can be transferred into the present and even into the future, so that our children and grandchildren do not have to suffer the torments that have swamped us for several decades.

In the meantime, enjoy this quiz book. The answers are given (although on a different page), so that those who wish to cheat may do so! But that is only kidding yourself. Come to think of it though, self-delusion has been a fairly visible facet of Scotland's national character through the ages, as far as football is concerned anyway. Enjoy the book!

David Potter
Kirkcaldy, 2015

Round

1

England

Scotland is fortunate in that our 'auld enemy' is not really an enemy at all. Other nations throughout the world are amazed at the amount of rhetoric and claptrap that Scotsmen and Englishmen can hurl at each other, in politics as well as football, without anyone getting shot! Admittedly, there have been a few 'nanas' on either side who used to indulge in the sport called football hooliganism, but all that proves is that the educational system on both sides of the border has a bit to go yet. There remains, in fact, a great deal of mutual respect for both nations, who together have won wars and built empires. Nevertheless, we do want to beat them!

1   The first five Scotland v. England internationals in England were played in 1873, 1875, 1877, 1879 and 1881 on a ground that is now famous for cricket. Which English county cricket club plays there now?

2   Why were games between Scotland and England played in England for three successive years from 1901 to 1903?

3   Until James McGrory in the 1930s, which Englishman held the world record for goal scoring?

4   Which famous Evertonian scored the 2 goals which beat Scotland 2–1 at Hampden in April 1927?

5   Which English goalkeeper had the same name (with a spelling variation) as a Scottish football team?

6   Which Englishman (who in later years lived in Edinburgh and supported Hearts) scored a late equaliser for England against Scotland at Hampden in 1956?

7   In Scotland's 3–9 defeat at Wembley in 1961, which Englishman scored a hat-trick?

8 When Scotland famously defeated England at Wembley
   in 1967, what was England's only change from their
   World Cup team of the previous year?

9 When Scotland beat England 2–0 at Hampden in 1974,
   which Englishman had the misfortune to score an own
   goal?

10 Which Englishman scored for England against Scotland
   at Wembley in April 1986, and then played a major
   part in Scottish domestic football for the rest of his
   footballing life?

11 Which Rangers player scored for England against Scotland
   at Wembley in 1996?

12 Who was the Scotsman who became assistant manager of
   England in 1996?

World Cup 1954

This was Scotland's first venture in the World Cup. They, like the rest of the British nations, had scorned the three World Cups before the Second World War (a shame, because Scotland might well have won it!), then unaccountably said that they would only go to the 1950 World Cup in Brazil if they were British champions. They came second in the Home International Championship, and that was the position they reached in 1954 as well, but this time accepted the invitation. Even then it was a half-hearted, amateurish business with players having to train in public parks wearing their own kit, and for the games themselves Scotland's jerseys were the thick ones that did such a fine job in December but were less suitable for Central Europe in June! One of the players recalls hearing the advice coming from the touchline which was, 'Come on Scotland! Get stuck in!' But it was at least a beginning, and for many people, including this 5 year old, their first acquaintance with television and a country called Uruguay.

1 In the run-up for this tournament, Scotland played one nation home and away in May 1954. Who was this?
2 Scotland played another game during the run-up in the stadium of the most recent Olympic Games. Where was this?
3 Why were no Rangers players in the squad?
4 How many men were in the Scotland squad to travel to Switzerland?
5 The first game was a respectable 0–1 defeat. Against whom?
6 In which city was this game played?
7 In Scotland's section there were four teams, but they only played two games. Who was the team that Scotland did NOT play?
8 Who was Scotland's team manager who announced before Scotland's game with Uruguay that he was resigning?
9 In these circumstances, it was hardly surprising that Scotland were on the wrong end of a heavy defeat. What was the score?
10 Two future Scotland managers were in the team that lost. Who were they?
11 In what city was this game played?
12 Who eventually won the World Cup this year?

Kenny Dalglish

Kenny Dalglish epitomised an era in Scottish football. Always the model professional – his name was conspicuously missing from those listed as troublemakers in Argentina in 1978 – Kenny was the man that most youngsters aspired to be. Often Scotland supporters felt that they didn't see him at his best, but one can still recall several brilliant goals. It was a shame that he did not do it more often, and it has to be admitted that he did have his disappointments with Scotland. There seems little doubt that Liverpool supporters saw better performances. How annoying!

1   How many caps did Kenny win?
2   In what year was he transferred from Celtic to Liverpool?
3   On what ground did he make his Scotland debut?
4   What team did he support as a boy?
5   Against whom did he play his last international on 12 November 1986?
6   How often did he win the European Cup as a player for Liverpool?

7   Which two English teams, other than Liverpool, did he manage?

8   He was interim manager for Celtic for a brief spell in 2000. In that time Celtic won the Scottish League Cup. Who did they beat in the final?

9   Against whom did Kenny score in the 1982 World Cup finals in Spain?

10 He signed for Celtic in 1967 but was farmed out to a junior team. Which team?

11 What was unusual about the goal that he scored against Ray Clements at Hampden in 1976?

12 How many goals did he score in total for Scotland?

The Nineteenth Century

We have cause to curse John Logie Baird and others for being so slow to invent television, videos and DVDs. Their tardiness has denied us the opportunity to see in action the valiant Scotsmen of the nineteenth century. This is a shame, for Scotland regularly beat England in 'The International' as it was called, and frequently deployed a weakened team to contemptuously beat Ireland and Wales. Without a shadow of a doubt, Scotland was the best footballing nation on the globe and would remain so well into the twentieth century. Pity it all went wrong, isn't it?

1   Where was the world's first international match played on 30 November 1872?
2   All Scotland's players came from one team. Which team?
3   Scotland's first trip to Wales was in 1877. They won 2–0, but at which ground?

4   In 1878, Scotland beat England 7–2 at the original
    Hampden Park. What feat did John McDougall of Vale of
    Leven achieve in this game?

5   What unparalleled feat did Scotland achieve from 1880 to
    1884?

6   In 1888, Scotland played their first home international
    outside Glasgow. Where?

7   In 1892, Tynecastle hosted its first international in a
    snowstorm. Who were the opponents?

8   In 1893, Scotland lost 2–5 to England at Richmond in
    London. Which future Queen of Great Britain was in
    attendance?

9   On 21 March 1896, Scotland defeated Wales 4–0 at a
    ground called Carolina Port. In which Scottish city is this
    ground?

10 On 4 April 1896, Scotland defeated England 2–1 at
   a dangerously overcrowded Celtic Park. What was
   significant and controversial about the make-up of the
   Scotland team?

11 Which Queen's Park player with the nickname of 'Toffee
   Bob', and whose name still appears frequently on British
   High Streets and retail centres, scored regularly for
   Scotland in the 1890s?

12 In what position did the legendary Ned Doig of Arbroath
   and Sunderland play?

Celtic Players

Often myths were circulated about Celtic players not being welcome to play for Scotland. This was sheer rubbish, but the selectors did nothing to dispel this rumour by ignoring the player featured in Question 4 whose total of caps seems grossly inadequate for his talents. The constant barracking of Celtic players like Jimmy Johnstone and Davie Hay by the less than well educated of the Rangers supporters didn't help either. It was a minority but an embarrassing one, which has now thankfully disappeared.

1   Who was the Celtic player who went missing in 1895 before the 0–3 defeat at Goodison Park to England?

2   Which two Celtic players scored the goals that beat England 2–0 at Hampden in April 1910?

3   In which city did John Thomson make his international debut for Scotland?

4   How many times did Jimmy McGrory play for Scotland?

5   Which three Celtic players played in the 1958 World Cup finals?

6   Which Celtic player was sent off in the World Cup game *v.* Czechoslovakia in May 1961?

7   Who in 1967 became the first Celtic player to score at Wembley?

8   How old was Ronnie Simpson when he made his international debut?

9   Who captained Scotland for the last time in the World Cup game against New Zealand in June 1982?

10   Which Celtic player was badly injured (contributing to a premature end of his career) after only 18 minutes of a friendly against Romania in March 2004?

11   Who is Celtic's most capped player for Scotland?

12   Which former Celtic player is the nephew of a former Scotland manager?

World Cup 1958

This was the World Cup for which all four British nations qualified. Sixteen teams were involved in the finals. This meant four groups of four, which meant a British team, a Western European team, an Eastern European team and a South American team in each group. It would be nice if it were so simple now! Scotland's run-up to the finals was chaotic and included a 0–4 hammering from England at Hampden in the rain in April. The answer to Question 5 (below) explains why Scotland were deprived of the manager of their choice, but does not explain why they failed to approach anyone else when Scott Symon of Rangers, Jimmy McGrory of Celtic or Tommy Walker of Hearts might have done the job on a temporary contract. Not surprisingly, managerless Scotland failed to live up to the expectations of the fans, more and more of whom now had televisions and could see the games, although, in practice, no Scotland game was shown live.

1 In one of Scotland's best ever performances, they beat
   Spain 4–2 at Hampden Park on 8 May 1957 in a World
   Cup qualifier. Which Dundee-born Blackpool player
   scored a hat-trick?

2 Why did the televising of Scotland's qualifier against
   Switzerland on 19 May 1957 from Basle cause some
   controversy in certain parts of the country?

3 Three days later, Scotland beat the World Cup holders in
   a friendly. Which country was this?

4 Scotland qualified on 6 November 1957 at Hampden.
   Whom did they defeat that day?

5 A tragic event in Germany in February 1958 deprived
   Scotland of their manager in the World Cup finals.
   Explain.

6 In what country were the World Cup finals held?

7 Who was the goalkeeper and captain of the Scotland
   side?

8   Who was the South African-born left-back in the first game?

9   The first game against Yugoslavia was Scotland's best performance. What was the score?

10 Against which South American team did Scotland play in the second game? It was their only (to date) encounter with this country.

11 Scotland's left-winger in the last game was James Imlach. For which English club did he play?

12 Which country eventually won this World Cup?

Ireland

Complicated by the fact that there are actually two Irelands in football terms, Scotland's relationship with the place has always been complex. In the early days, Scotland were well ahead of Ireland, but this was because football in Ireland was not the obsession that it was in Scotland. One feels that both Irelands (the North and the South) should be handicapped by a weak domestic structure, but when their 'wild geese' come together for an international now there is a determination to succeed that Scotland would do well to copy.

1 In which year did Scotland first play Ireland?
2 Several times Scotland have played against Ireland at the home of Cliftonville. It sounds a very lonely place. What is it called?
3 In 1901, at Celtic Park, Scotland beat Ireland by a record score. What was it?
4 In what year did Ireland beat Scotland for the first time ever?

5 In 1920, Scotland beat Ireland 3–0 at Celtic Park. Who was the Celtic player who played for Ireland that day?

6 Who scored 5 goals for Scotland against Ireland in Belfast in 1929?

7 Which Celtic player, with the name of a bird, played for and captained Northern Ireland several times in the 1950s?

8 Who was the Northern Ireland Internationalist who scored Rangers' only goal in the Scottish League Cup final of 1957/58?

9 In what year did Scotland play Eire for the first time?

10 Which Scottish goalkeeper saved a penalty for Scotland in Belfast in October 1967?

11 On 1 June 1977, Scotland beat Northern Ireland 3–0. The Irish team contained two men who would in later years manage teams in Scotland. Who?

12 In what year was the British Home International Championship played for the last time?

Hampden

On Hampden's battlefield,
The results will be revealed,
The Saxon foe will yield,
And England's fate will be sealed!

Hampden (or the National Stadium, as some call it), may well have had its critics – and it certainly had its imperfections – but everyone over a certain age has his or her own memories of teeming terracings and pipe-band music (and usually loads of rain!) before the start of Internationals or Cup finals! It is now a very modern all-seater stadium with about a third of the capacity it once had, but one still cannot fail to be impressed by the sheer majesty of the grand old lady with its excellent museum and cafeteria. There has been quite a lot of football played there!

1 There have been three Hampdens. When was the ground on the current site opened?
2 What is the nearest railway station to Hampden Park?
3 In what year was the first Scotland v. England International played at the current Hampden Park?
4 In 1914, Scotland beat England 3–1 at Hampden. Which Rangers player has the honour of scoring the last goal in a Hampden International before the Great War?
5 In what year did Hampden see Scotland's first defeat to England at the ground?
6 What was the first Hampden Roar?
7 There was also at one point a Hampden Bowl. What was that?
8 What record did Hampden set up in April 1937?
9 When was the first International game at Hampden televised?

10 Since 1956, every Scotland v. England game at Hampden has been televised live, except one. In which year was the game not televised live?

11 During the 1950s and '60s, what was the official attendance limit for Hampden?

12 Renovations at Hampden took some considerable time in the 1990s, and Scotland had to play games elsewhere. Apart from obvious venues in Glasgow, Edinburgh and Aberdeen, where else did Scotland play some home games during this period?

North of the Tay

It is often erroneously assumed that Scottish football centres on Glasgow and the immediate surrounding area. Not so! Tayside, Deeside and the Highlands – less densely populated areas than the Central Belt – have nevertheless produced many great players for their country, and provide a large amount of fans for the Tartan Army.

1   Which member of Hibs Famous Five spent his early years in Montrose and went on to win 18 caps for Scotland?

2   Who was the Coupar Angus-born man who scored the only goal in Scotland's 1–0 defeat of England in April 1964?

3   What was the name of the burly full-back who played for Aberdeen and earned 10 caps for Scotland in the 1920s?

4   Alec Troup, who earned 5 caps for Scotland, played for Forfar Athletic and Dundee before, during and after the

Great War. To which English team was he transferred in
January 1923 before returning to Dundee in 1930?

5 On Wednesday, 2 December 1936, Scotland lost 1–2 to
Wales at Dens Park. But the crowd was buzzing with
rumours about a major event that was soon to shake
British society. What was the event?

6 Who was the Aberdeen player who scored a great goal
for Scotland in the 1–1 draw with England at Hampden in
1956, and repeated the feat in 1960 when the score was
the same?

7 Who is the only man to have managed both Scotland and
Dundee United?

8 Who was the Dundee United forward who played
   20 times for Scotland and had the nickname 'Luggy'?

9 Where was Peter Lorimer of Leeds United born?

10 Gordon Strachan played for two clubs north of the River
   Tay. Which two?

11 Willie Miller and Alex McLeish played together for a long
   time, both with Aberdeen and Scotland. Which of the
   two earned the more caps?

12 Which Scotland cap of the 1990s was born in Fort
   William?

Round
10

World Cup 1974

Arguably, this was Scotland's best ever World Cup final campaign. They certainly returned undefeated and enjoyed universal support back home and even in England whose supporters (to a large extent) jumped ship and supported Scotland, their own team having failed to qualify. The team was tolerably well disciplined and well managed and only failed to qualify by a whisker. It might have been different if the manager had deployed either Denis Law or Jimmy Johnstone in the last game, who were both with the squad and might have been able to snatch a vital late goal through their sheer virtuosity.

1   Which country did Scotland beat twice home and away in their qualifying campaign in autumn 1972?
2   Scotland beat Czechoslovakia 2–1 in September 1973 to qualify for the finals. Who were the scorers?
3   Who was the manager?
4   Which country beat England in the World Cup qualifying campaign that year?

5 In the Home International Championships before the World Cup finals began, Scotland lost to one of the British nations. Which one?

6 Where were the World Cup finals held in 1974?

7 Scotland's first game was against Zaire. Both Scotland's goals in the 2–0 match were scored by men who played for the same club. Which club?

8 Who was the Hibs player who played in this game?

9 In the game against Brazil, Scotland were generally admitted to be the better side in the 0–0 draw, but Scotland's captain missed a chance which haunted him for the rest of his life. Who was he?

10 The final game was played against a country that no longer exists. What was it?

11 The game ended in a 1–1 draw. Scotland's goal came in the last minute. Who scored it?

12 Who won the World Cup that year?

Round

II

Wales

Wales is a country to which we feel a natural affinity. There is a tendency for them to prefer rugby rather than football and every two years when they come to Edinburgh to play against Scotland at Murrayfield, they bring with them a good atmosphere and make many friends in the city and surrounding area. In football terms, they probably have a worse record than Scotland, but they have, nevertheless, produced many fine players over the years and will continue to do so. Most of us regret with nostalgia the passing of the Home International Championship, not least because it gave Scotland a chance to visit Cardiff every two years.

1   Scotland's record defeat of Wales was on 23 March 1878. What was the score?
2   Wales beat Scotland for the first time in Scotland in 1906. On what ground was the game played?
3   Who was the legendary Welshman of the Edwardian era

who played for Manchester City and Manchester United and scored for Wales against Scotland in 1905?

4   Which of the following Scottish grounds has NOT staged a Scotland v. Wales game? Celtic Park, Tannadice, Tynecastle, Dens Park or Pittodrie?

5   Scotland played Wales on 25 May 2011. In which city was the game played?

6   On 3 May 1969, Scotland beat Wales 5–3 at Wrexham. What was significant about this game?

7   On what famous occasion did Wales play Scotland in England?

8   In 1997, Wales beat Scotland 1–0. Their goal was scored by a man who would later take part in Scottish domestic football. Who?

9   What was the surname of the two legendary brothers, John and Mel, who played for Wales in the 1950s?

10 Who scored a hat-trick for Scotland against Wales at Ibrox on 27 October 1928?

11 And who scored a hat-trick for Wales against Scotland at the Millenium Stadium, Cardiff on 18 February 2004?

12 Which Manchester City full-back, playing for Scotland, scored a hideous own goal at Hampden on 17 May 1978?

Round

12

1900–1914

The early years of the twentieth century were good ones for Scottish football. It was the time of the outstanding Celtic team of Willie Maley, and in England, the time of the great days of Newcastle United. Both teams supplied many players for Scotland, but the talent seemed virtually limitless with most teams in England having at least a sprinkling of Scottish talent. Away from football, great changes were being made with the election of the Liberals in 1906 (under Glaswegian Henry Campbell-Bannerman) a clear sign that social progress now had to be made. But even in 1914, poverty remained a huge issue in Scotland, in spite of all its heavy industry, and problems like alcohol and crime were rampant. But, thank heavens, there was football!

1   At which ground did Scotland open the twentieth century on 3 February 1900 with a 5–2 defeat of Wales?

2   Which famous politician sponsored the 1900 Scotland v.
     England International at Celtic Park, donating his racing
     colours of yellow and brown for Scotland to wear?

3   Which player, whose name now appears on many
     High Street shops, scored a hat-trick for Scotland that day?

4   In Scotland's record 11–0 defeat of Ireland on
     23 February 1901 at Celtic Park, there were two Scottish
     players of the same name, one who played for Celtic and
     one who played for Rangers. What was the name?

5   Which ground staged its first and only International as
     Scotland defeated Wales 5–1 on 15 March 1902?

6   The Ibrox Disaster occurred in April 1902. Who was
     the 'Blue Streak' who played for Aston Villa at the time
     (subsequently playing for Celtic and Kilmarnock), and
     who may have inadvertently caused the disaster as the
     crowd swayed to see him charge down the wing?

7   Where was the 1907 England v. Scotland International played in a vain attempt to attract a larger crowd of Scotsmen?

8   Which Celtic player was nicknamed 'the uncrowned king of Ireland' after scoring 4 goals for Scotland in Dublin in 1908?

9   In Scotland's 2–0 defeat of England on 2 April 1910, the forward line read Bennett, McMenemy, Quinn, Higgins and Templeton. In what way was Sandy Higgins the odd man out?

10 What was the surname of the Newcastle United player nicknamed 'Peter the Great' who was badly injured while captaining Scotland against Wales at Cardiff in March 1911?

11 Between 1900 and 1914, England beat Scotland only once in our home country. What year was that?

12 For what team, no longer is existence, did the famous goalkeeper Jimmy Brownlie play?

Denis Law

Denis Law was always a controversial character. He never played in Scottish domestic football, and occasionally caused offence by his feigned insouciance after a poor performance with Scotland. But this was merely a façade. There was no more committed or determined Scottish patriot that Denis Law, and he had many fine performances for his country, even though on occasion one got the impression that his clubs in England and Italy were reluctant to release him to play for Scotland. Famously, on the awful day that England won the World Cup in July 1966, Denis was playing golf!

1   In which Scottish city was he born?
2   What was his first professional football club?
3   In 1958, he became Scotland's youngest player in modern times. Who was the opposition?
4   In 1961, when with Manchester City, he scored 6 goals against Luton Town. But something unusual subsequently happened. What was that?

5   He subsequently joined an Italian team. Which?

6   In 1963, he won an English Cup medal for Manchester
     United, scoring in the final. Who were the opposition
     during this match?

7   On two occasions he scored 4 goals for Scotland at
     Hampden. Name either of the teams against whom he
     performed this feat.

8   In which two successive years did he score for Scotland
     against England at Wembley?

9   Injury forced him to miss a particularly important fixture
     for his club in 1968. What was the fixture?

10   To which team did he move in 1973?

11   Who was the TV commentator who famously forgot
     his neutrality and shouted, 'Come on, Denis!' when
     Denis broke through in the World Cup qualifier against
     Czechoslovakia in September 1973?

12   His last game in professional football was an International
     for Scotland. Who were the opposition?

World Cup 1978

Oh, Argentina! In the long and lamentable catalogue of Scottish fiascos, this one ranks among the foremost. A brilliant qualifying campaign was followed by a sustained period of optimism and euphoria which lasted all through winter 1977/78, and the feel-good factor was not dented by some awful performances in the Home International Championship. No sooner had they landed in Argentina than we heard the moans about accommodation, the salacious scandals gleefully related and exaggerated by the press and, more damagingly, the stories of internal discord. The collapse was then humiliating and total, and included a dope scandal. Nor was the disgrace entirely mitigated by one good performance in the last game. There was a song at the time made popular by Julie Covington from the Eva Peron musical. It was called 'Don't Cry For Me, Argentina!' and it was difficult to refrain from tears during this disgraceful episode from which only a handful of players emerged with any kind of credit.

1   Along with Wales, who was the other team in Scotland's qualifying section?

2   Scotland qualified for the finals by beating Wales. Where was this game played?

3   Scotland's manager was Ally MacLeod. With which Glasgow team did he play from 1949–55 and then 1963–64?

4   Which well-known Scottish comedian recorded a song that began with the lyrics 'We're on the march with Ally's army'?

5   Virtually on the eve of departure for Argentina, Scotland played England at Hampden. What was the score?

6   The first game was against Peru and Scotland scored first. Who scored the goal?

7   Which player missed a penalty in this game?

8   Which Scotland player tested positive for drugs after the game and was sent home?

9   For which English team did this man play at the time?

10 Scotland next played Iran. What was unusual about Scotland's goal in the 1–1 draw?

11 Everyone knows of Archie Gemmill's great goal against Holland. He also scored a penalty in the 3–2 win, but who scored the other goal?

12 Who eventually won the 1978 World Cup?

Picture Round

1 This is a picture taken of a Scotland squad at training around 1961. Who is the manager on the left-hand side?
2 The two men next to him share the same surname. What is it?
3 Denis Law is in this picture. Where is he?
4 And where is Jim Baxter?

5 This picture was taken after a famous Scottish victory in 1967. Where?

6 In the front is the man said to be the cornerstone of this victory. Who is he?

7 The man with the England shirt on is actually a Scotland player who has just changed shirts with an English opponent. He played for an English club, however. Who is he?

8 The man at the back whose face is partially hidden will soon win a European Cup medal with Celtic. Who is he?

9 In what year was this photograph taken? Clue – it was
   before a particularly tragic event.
10 Why is there, apparently, no goalkeeper?

11 Who is the famous Scotland player and captain seated on
    the right in this picture?

12 Who is this famous Scotland player and captain in the 1950s?

Edinburgh Players

Edinburgh is sometimes looked upon as a non-football city. This is unfair, for the capital has provided loads of players for Scotland. Yet even the most ardent of 'burgers' (Edinburgers, as distinct from 'weegies' i.e. Glaswegians) would have to admit that the record of the two teams, Hearts and Hibs, has been somewhat disappointing to their many fans. The dismal practice of selling star players at times when they did not really need to has contributed to the air of depression that hangs over Edinburgh's teams sometimes. There is even the fear of getting a really good player, for their supporters know in their heart of Hearts (oops! Sorry!) that sooner or later, he will be sold. But then again, there is always the castle, the rugby, the cricket and Edinburgh Festival as well in that beautiful city.

I   Which Hearts centre forward famously hit the bar late in the 1950 game against England at Hampden, thus depriving Scotland of their opportunity to go to the 1950 World Cup finals?

2　All of Hibs 'Famous Five' forwards played for Scotland. Which one of them went on to manage Scotland?

3　Who was the Hibs player who was one of the Wembley Wizards?

4　There were two great Hearts players by the name of Walker. What was the Christian name of the earlier one, sometimes nicknamed 'Houdini'?

5　In the 2–0 win over Latvia in Riga in October 1996, I goal was scored by an ex-Hibs player and the other by a current Hibs player. Who were they?

6　Who was the fair-haired Hearts and Aston Villa player who played 18 times for Scotland during the interwar period between 1919 and 1939?

7　Other than Hearts and Hibs, which two Edinburgh teams have supplied players for Scotland?

8　Who was the famous Hearts goalkeeper who played in

the Wembley Wizards side and in later years wrote for
the *Sunday Post*?

9 Who are the three men who have managed both Hearts
   and Scotland?

10 What nickname did Laurie Reilly earn after his exploits at
   Wembley in 1953?

11 Who was the Hibs full-back who captained Scotland
   for one game in 1946 before losing the captaincy to his
   brother in 1947?

12 A player called Begbie played for Hearts and Scotland in
   the 1890s. What was his Christian name?

1919–1939

After 1919, there were meant to be no more wars. Sadly that was not the case, because not enough thought and rather too much spite and venom had been put into the Treaty of Versailles. This guaranteed the humiliation of Germany until the country found a leader who would lead them to have another go. The economy was always a major problem. There was huge unemployment even when Labour came to power, and the party then confounded their supporters by joining ranks with the capitalists to form a National Government when the crisis became too bad. It was a fine period for Scottish football, though, and on several occasions one could have said, quite truthfully, that Scotland was the best in the world. Domestically, Rangers won most honours but Celtic and Motherwell both had their moments as well.

1 In the interwar years, Scotland lost only twice to England at Hampden. In which two years?
2 In the very first official International after the Great War, Scotland drew 1–1 with Wales in Cardiff in February

1920. Scotland's goal scorer was nicknamed 'Tireless Tommy'. What was his name?

3 Between March 1920 and April 1923, one player scored for Scotland in every International bar one – a total of ten games. Who was this prolific goal scorer?

4 Which Scottish international left-winger was transferred from Dundee to Everton in early 1923?

5 Who was the Raith Rovers centre half who captained Scotland to wins over all three home countries in 1925?

6 In May 1930, Scotland beat France 2–0 in Paris. Who scored both goals?

7 Who was the Scottish Prime Minister of Great Britain who attended the Scotland v. England International at Hampden in 1931?

8 The 'Hampden Roar' was said to have been born in 1933 when Scotland scored the winning goal against England.

The goal came from a Rangers-Celtic combination. Who passed to whom?

9 Scotland lost at Wembley in 1930, 1932 and 1934. Who was the record goal-scoring Celtic centre forward who, incredibly, was not chosen on any of these occasions?

10 In 1935, Scotland beat England 2–0 with 2 goals from Douglas Duncan of Derby County. What was his nickname?

11 Shortly after the Berlin Olympics of 1936, the Führer suffered another humiliation at Ibrox on 14 October 1936 when his German team were defeated by Scotland. Who scored the 2 goals in Scotland's victory?

12 When Scotland beat England 1–0 at Wembley in 1938, who was the famous future manager of a well-known English team who played at right half?

World Cup 1982

In this World Cup, Scotland managed to regain some respectability. The squad was better disciplined and played some good football in the heat of the Spanish sun, with, as in 1974, qualification to the knock-out stages depending on the last game. Unlike 1978, Scotland could return home with their heads held high. The atmosphere engendered by the Scottish and Brazilian fans when they met will be long remembered.

1   Who was Scotland's manager at this time?
2   Scotland began their campaign with a 1–0 win in Sweden in September 1980. Which future Scotland manager scored the only goal of the game?
3   Scotland qualified in October 1981 with a 0–0 draw. Against whom?

4 Which geopolitical event, just before the World Cup started, might have prevented Scotland's participation in the finals of this World Cup?

5 In which two Spanish cities did Scotland play their games?

6 Against whom did Scotland begin their campaign, winning 5–2?

7 In this game, a Scottish player had the same surname as a country in the World Cup. Who was he?

8 Scotland then lost 1–4 to Brazil. Who scored Scotland's goal?

9 Who was the English commentator who crassly described this goal as a 'toe-poke'?

10 In Scotland's final game with a 2–2 draw against the USSR, who opened the scoring for Scotland?

11 Who were the two defenders who famously collided with each other in the build-up for the crucial goal for the USSR?

12 Which country eventually won the World Cup?

Wembley

Wembley! Deliberately built by the triumphalist British in the early 1920s to be the best sporting stadium in the world following the Great War, it has retained this reputation for most of its life, the home of England Internationals and English Cup finals. Some of Scotland's greatest triumphs have happened there – from the Wembley Wizards in 1928 onwards – and there used to be a biennial exodus from Scotland for the 'Wembley weekend'. Sadly, too many of them ended up in failure and disappointment, but there were also the sights of London to savour, as well as a great deal of drink!

1 Scotland first played at Wembley in 1924. What was the score?

2 In the famous Wembley Wizards game of 1928, who scored a hat-trick?

3 Who was the player, famous for wearing baggy pants, who played at inside left that day?

4 In 1936 who was the Hearts player (who later became their manager) who equalised for Scotland from a penalty kick, taking his time to replace the ball several times after the wind blew it off the spot?

5 Who was the Morton goalkeeper who distinguished himself at Wembley in 1949 and 1951, but particularly 1949?

6 Infamously, Scotland lost 3–9 to England in 1961. Can you name any of Scotland's three goal scorers?

7 Who scored both of Scotland's goals (one via the penalty spot) in the 2–1 win in 1963?

8 In 1967, Scotland became the first team to beat England after their World Cup success in 1966. What was the score?

9 Can you name one of Scotland's scorers that day?

10 Who was the goalkeeper unfairly blamed for Scotland's 1–5 defeat in 1975?

11 On 4 June 1977, Scotland beat England 2–1. It was the day of the infamous breaking of the goalposts by triumphant Scotland fans. What other (non-footballing) event was being celebrated in Great Britain that weekend?

12 In November 1999, Scotland beat England in a European Championship Qualifier. Who scored Scotland's goal in the 1–0 victory?

1946–1980

The Welfare State and the National Health Service arrived in the late 1940s, and although the effects were not immediate, by the end of the 1950s everyone was talking about 'the affluent society'. Never again would poverty be a major problem, although the 1970s was definitely a decade of industrial unrest. Football continued to be the main Scottish obsession, and domestically Hibs, Hearts, Aberdeen and Dundee all had their moments of glory. Rangers were always consistently there, but Celtic's European Cup triumph of 1967 was Scottish football's finest hour. Yet the seeds of decline were sown by Scottish clubs all too ready to sell their star players, pursuing immediate greed rather than long-term thinking about team building. Immediately after crossing the border, some players began to lose interest in playing for Scotland.

I   Who scored the only goal of the game in the Victory International against England at Hampden Park in April 1946?

2   Who was the East Fife player who scored a hat-trick for Scotland on his debut in 1949 and was never again capped?

3   Which country in December 1950 became the first overseas country to defeat Scotland at Hampden?

4   What virtually unprecedented event occurred at Hampden Park on 8 May 1963?

5   Many people felt that the Wales v. Scotland game at Ninian Park on 22 October 1966 should not have been played. Why?

6   Who in 1967 scored an infamous own goal for Scotland fifteen days before winning the European Cup?

7   Scotland drew 1–1 with West Germany at Hampden in a World Cup qualifier in April 1969. Who scored Scotland's late equaliser?

8   Scotland and England drew 0–0 in 1970. When was the only previous time that there had been a goalless draw between these two countries?

9   Where did Scotland go to play in a tournament in
    summer 1972?

10 In February 1973, Scotland ill-advisedly played a game
    against England at Hampden to celebrate the centenary of
    the Scottish Football Association. What was the score?

11 In May 1976, Scotland won the Home International
    Championship by beating Wales, Northern Ireland and
    England. Who was Scotland's goalkeeper in all three
    games?

12 Scotland played a friendly against World Cup champions
    Argentina at Hampden in June 1979. Who scored
    Argentina's third goal in their 3–1 victory?

World Cup 1986

Once again Scotland maintained their impressive record of qualification, but once again they returned home (as in 1974 and 1982) with a 'hard luck' story of good performances, narrow defeats but no progress to the knock-out stages. The team was managed by Alec Ferguson on a temporary basis and in tandem with his permanent job at Aberdeen. The finals had twenty-four teams in this year and some of the best-placed thirds could qualify. Sadly, Scotland could not even do that.

1   Where were the 1986 World Cup finals held?
2   Against whom did Jim Bett score a late goal to give Scotland a somewhat undeserved victory in the qualifying section on 28 May 1985?
3   In the final qualifying game against Wales, why did Scotland have to exchange goalkeepers at half-time?
4   Who scored the late penalty that gave Scotland a draw in that game?

5   Which tragic event overshadowed this game?

6   Scotland had to play a play-off before qualifying for the finals. Against whom?

7   Graeme Souness was captain of Scotland in the first two games in the World Cup finals. After the finals he would become player-manager of Rangers, but for which team had he played the previous season?

8   Who scored Scotland's goal in the 1–2 defeat by West Germany?

9   Jose Batista of Uruguay played little part in the 0–0 draw against Scotland. Why was that?

10 A total of five Dundee United players took part in the finals. Can you name them?

11 Who was Scotland's goalkeeper in all three games?

12 Who eventually won the World Cup?

Rangers Players

Scotland was rocked when Rangers went into administration on 14 February 2012. Rangers, like them or lump them, were a huge Scottish institution who supplied so many players to the national team. They were not always popular with supporters of other clubs, who despised them for their shameful policy of religious segregation (something that astonished English visitors), became increasingly suspicious of their financial deals, and feared a visit from their supporters – some of whom did little to dispel their nickname of the 'Huns'. Nevertheless, their contribution to Scottish football has been huge. It is even possible to feel a certain amount of pity and nostalgia for them. Certainly they have had many fine players who have also played well for Scotland.

1   Who was the Rangers player with the Biblical name who, in 1876, became the first Ranger to be capped for Scotland?

2 Which Rangers member played for Scotland in the 1890s and had a son who was one of the Wembley Wizards of 1928?

3 Which Rangers left-winger was known as the 'Wee Blue Devil'?

4 Which Rangers captain played for Scotland in the 1930s and had a son who played for Celtic and was also capped for Scotland in the 1960s?

5 Which Rangers goalkeeper became Scotland's manager?

6 In Scotland's 3–9 thrashing at Wembley in 1961, who were the two Rangers full-backs?

7 In October 1961, Scotland beat Northern Ireland 6–1 in Belfast. All the goals were scored by three Rangers players. Who were they?

8 Which Rangers player broke his leg at Wembley in 1963?

9 Against whom did John Greig score a famous goal for Scotland in November 1965 at Hampden in a World Cup qualifier?

10 Who was the only Rangers player playing in the game against Holland in Argentina 1978?

11 Which Rangers player scored a goal against Scotland in 1996?

12 How many goals did Ally McCoist score for Scotland?

Managers

There can be little doubt that the job of Scotland manager is one of the most poisoned of chalices even in the troubled world of football managing, a career not always characterised by professional longevity. An international manager has a particularly difficult task in that he lies idle for months on end, then suddenly is called upon to produce the goods only to be frequently frustrated by players abruptly, with the full and sometimes blatant encouragement of their clubs, becoming 'injured' or 'unavailable' for an important International fixture! Scotland's managers really do deserve our sympathy and support!

1   Who was the manager who suddenly resigned in the middle of the 1954 World Cup finals?
2   Who was the manager when Scotland beat England three years in a row from 1962 to 1964?
3   Which Kilmarnock manager took over the Scotland job on an interim basis in season 1966–67?

4 Which Scottish manager has the same surname as a Scottish county?

5 Jock Stein was manager of Scotland from 1978 until 1985. He had previously been manager on a part-time basis. In what year was that?

6 Jock died at Cardiff in September 1985 at the end of a Wales v. Scotland World Cup qualifier. What was the score that night?

7 Who took over on a short-term contract until the end of the 1986 World Cup?

8 Who was Scotland's manager during the European Championships in England in 1996?

9 Which famous German Internationalist became manager of Scotland in 2002?

10 Which team did Alex McLeish leave Scotland to become manager of in 2007?

11 There have been two Scotland managers called Brown. What are their Christian names?

12 Who left the Scotland job suddenly in 1972 to become manager of Manchester United?

World Cup 1990

This World Cup was a rollercoaster of emotion, but it was also a classic piece of Scottish self-destruction beginning with a horrible defeat to an incredulous Costa Rica side as Scotland, not for the first time, became the laughing stock of world football. To their credit, Scotland rallied and brought off a good win against Sweden, but never really shrugged off the handicap of that dreadful first defeat which really called into question Scotland's credibility as a footballing nation. It was, however, some sort of achievement to qualify for the World Cup finals five times in a row, and the supporters, now beginning to be called the Tartan Army, were a credit to their country.

1   Who was Scotland's manager at the time of the 1990 World Cup?
2   In what country was it played?
3   Scotland's captain in all three games was Roy Aitken. Which club was he playing for at the time?

4 Arguably Scotland's worst ever defeat in World Cup history came in the 1990 World Cup at the hands of a little-known Central American country called Costa Rica. What does Costa Rica mean in English?

5 In the qualifying section, Scotland beat Cyprus 3–2 in Cyprus. What was slightly controversial about Scotland's winner scored by Richard Gough?

6 In the game which finally decided that Scotland would qualify for the finals, they were leading 1–0 at Hampden but then lost a dreadful own goal late in the game, causing anxiety for the supporters in the last few minutes. Who were the opposition?

7 In the warm-up games for the finals, Scotland played a game at Pittodrie against a team they had never played before and sustained an appalling defeat. Who were the opposition?

8 In the game that Scotland played against Sweden on 16 June, which somewhat controversial character scored a penalty for Scotland?

9 In that game, two future Scotland managers played for Scotland. Who were they?

10 That game also saw a Norwich City player in Scotland's colours. Who was he?

11 Scotland went out of the tournament by losing their final game 0–1. Who were the opposition?

12 Who eventually won the 1990 World Cup?

1981–2000

These were years of a gradual decline of Scotland's national team from respectability to insignificance, which occasionally included becoming a laughing stock. There were some good moments as well, but there seems little doubt that the explosion of a grotesque amount of money in football in the 1990s was something that, for some reason or other, Scotland did not come out of very well. Domestic football declined to an almost frightening extent, yet Scotland retained its record of having the highest percentage per head of its population that attended a football match every weekend. Off the field, computers and technology took hold, and the Thatcherite decade of the 1980s had its reaction, which included the opening of a Scottish Parliament in Edinburgh in 1999.

1   John Robertson scored the penalty that beat England at Wembley in May 1981. But which John Robertson? Was it the one who played for Hearts or the one who played for Notts Forest?

2   Who scored in his Scotland debut against Switzerland at Hampden in March 1983?

3   Which Commonwealth country did Scotland tour in summer 1983, winning all three games played?

4   When Scotland played England in 1985, it was no longer for the Home International Championship, it was for a trophy named after a famous English footballing administrator and statesman. Who?

5   Scotland won this game 1–0. Which Dundee United player scored the goal?

6   Which country beat Scotland for the first time at Hampden in a European Qualifier in February 1987?

7   Why did Gary MacKay of Hearts become the toast of Ireland in November 1987?

8   Scotland broke new ground in February 1988 when they earned a 2–2 draw in a country where they had never played before. Where was this?

9 In March 1990, Scotland beat the World Cup holders 1–0 at Hampden in a friendly. Who was this?

10 In April 1993, Scotland sustained a real hammering, losing 0–5 to a European nation, which questioned Scotland's credibility. Who were the opponents?

11 In summer 1995 in the Kirin Cup, Scotland drew 0–0 with the host nation. In which city, well known for dark events earlier in the century, did this game take place?

12 On 28 April 1999, Scotland scored a rare away win against a team reckoned to be one of the best in the world. Who was this?

European Championships

Scotland's record in this tournament is, frankly, a disgrace. We were reluctant to enter it in the early stages, and we have qualified only twice. Our terrible performances have been a major loss, for although there are many fine teams in Europe and it is difficult to imagine Scotland winning the trophy, nevertheless it would be nice to take part – and there are the precedents of Denmark in 1992 and Greece in 2004!

1   Scotland have qualified only twice for the European Championships, in 1992 and 1996. Where was the first of these finals tournaments played?
2   Who was Scotland's manager in 1992?
3   Who was the captain in that year, and reputed not to have enjoyed the best of relationships with the manager?

4 Scotland lost their first game in the 1992 European
   Championship finals 0–1 to Holland. Who was the Dutch
   goal scorer who, like Jimmy Johnstone, had a pathological
   fear of flying?

5 Scotland's team against Germany on 15 June 1992 was
   a recognisably Scottish one, in that eight of the starting
   eleven had names beginning with 'Mc'. Name one of the
   three who didn't.

6 The last game was against a team called the CIS
   (Commonwealth of Independent States). Who were
   they?

7 Which Aberdeen player scored the only goal of the
   game against Finland in a tense qualifier for the 1996
   Euro Championships at Hampden in September 1995?

8 In the run-up to Euro 96, Scotland played two games
   in the USA. They lost both. The first was to the USA
   themselves, but who did they lose to in Miami on
   29 May 1996?

9 Scotland's first game in Eur 96 was a creditable 0–0 draw
   against Holland. Where was this game played?

10 Everyone remembers the 0–2 defeat to England at
   Wembley. Who scored the first England goal?

11 In the final game against Switzerland, who scored
   Scotland's only goal in the 1–0 victory?

12 Why did Scotland supporters suddenly and
   uncharacteristically find themselves cheering on England
   that night?

The Twenty-First Century

The twenty-first century saw another stage in Scotland's apparently irreversible decline, and is something which causes the Tartan Army a great deal of distress. Yet Scotland is a small nation, and we are possibly now at the place where small nations should be. The trouble is that we have known better and we demand better of our players. This is the way that it ought to be, and we should continue to insist on the total elimination of national humiliations and (the possibly more insidious) 'glorious failures' which have permeated our past. Arise, Scotland, arise!

1   Who was Scotland's manager as the new millennium dawned in January 2000?

2   Which player in March 2001 played two games within six days of each other at Hampden, winning a Scottish League Cup medal for Celtic on the Sunday and earning a

draw against Scotland the following Saturday?

3 Who was surprisingly appointed as Scotland's manager in early 2002?

4 In September 2002, in what was freely referred to as Scotland's worst ever performance, to whom were Scotland 0–2 down at half-time before coming back to earn a far from respectable draw?

5 Scotland made it to the play-offs for the European Championships of 2004. They beat Holland 1–0 at Hampden in the first leg. Who scored the goal?

6 What was the score in the second leg?

7 In 2006, Scotland won a trophy! What was it called?

8 In autumn 2006 and 2007, Scotland beat the World Cup runners-up home and away, 1–0 in both cases. Who was that?

9 Name the two men with Rangers connections who

became managers of Scotland in the 2000s.

10 Gordon Strachan was appointed manager of Scotland in 2013. How many caps did he earn as a player?

11 Scotland opened their qualifying campaign for the 2014 World Cup with a dismal 0–0 draw at home. Against whom?

12 Which qualifier for the World Cup in Brazil 2014 did Scotland beat both home and away in the qualifying group?

Anglo-Scots

It is a sad fact of Scotland that talented Scottish people often make a bigger impact in England than they do in Scotland. Football is no exception in this regard, and the past 150 years have seen a constant haemorrhaging of talent southwards as rascally Scottish clubs have seen this as a way to make a fast buck, and the players themselves have found the 'streets paved with gold' myth hard to resist. Not all have been a success, but many have. This is a 'Who Am I?' round.

1   I was born in the Highlands and was arguably Newcastle United's best ever player. My nickname was 'Peter the Great'.

2   I sadly committed suicide by jumping in front of a train in 1957.

3   I was one of Hibs' 'Famous Five' but also played for Manchester City.

4   I played a few games for Celtic but most of my playing career was with Preston North End. I both captained and managed Scotland.

5   I played for Motherwell, but then I moved to Liverpool where I was part of the great success of the 1960s. I have a religious name.

6   I started playing with St Mirren, but the bulk of my footballing life was in England, and my goal in Argentina is often called Scotland's best ever goal.

7   My English team was Tottenham Hotspur, but I was still with Dundee when I scored my most famous goal at Hampden against England in 1964.

8   I was born in Aberdeen, but I never played club football in Scotland. My first English team was Huddersfield Town.

9   I was born in Stirling and played for Leeds United. Many people didn't like my somewhat robust style of play.

10   I was a goalkeeper for Arsenal, and became a BBC pundit.

11   I once famously missed a penalty at Wembley but I had a good career with several English teams, notably Leeds United and Liverpool.

12   I am the only Scottish cap ever to have played for Livingston and Norwich City.

World Cup 1998

Craig Brown has reason to be proud of his team in this World Cup finals, the last that Scotland have played in to date. A luckless and creditable defeat in the opening game of the tournament was followed by an equally creditable draw with Norway. This meant that it all depended on the last game. Hopes were high, but Scotland seemed once again to obey the unwritten law that Scotland are sometimes allowed to get to the World Cup finals, but cannot thereafter make any further progress. They once again 'blew up'. The country was once again plunged into dismay, and when Scotland failed to qualify for subsequent World Cup finals, it was almost a relief!

I   Scotland's qualifying campaign for the 1998 World Cup was characterised by astonishing events in October 1996 when a team refused to play Scotland because of a dispute about floodlights. Which team?

2 FIFA, equally astonishingly, declared that the game should be played again on a neutral ground. Where was the game eventually played?

3 One of Scotland's best performances in the qualifying campaign was against Austria at Celtic Park when they won 2–0. Who scored both goals?

4 Scotland's game against Belarus at Pittodrie was scheduled for 6 September 1997 but was in fact played a day later on 7 September. Why?

5 Scotland eventually qualified by beating Latvia 2–0. Where?

6 Scotland had the honour of opening the tournament by playing the defending champions. Who was this?

7 Which Scotland player scored a penalty in this game?

8 Which Scotland player had the misfortune to score an own goal?

9 Scotland then drew 1–1 with Norway. A future Rangers player was playing for Norway. Who?

10 And there was also a future Celtic player as well. Who?

11 Against which country did Scotland collapse feebly 0–3 in their final game?

12 Which Scotland player was sent off in this game?

Records

'More records than Andy Stewart', was a phrase frequently employed about Scotland's ability to make an impact on the world scene. Not all records are good ones and, in addition, some of them are difficult to prove or have to be qualified with phrases like 'World Cup' or 'domestic' added. Nevertheless, they are good for arguing about!

1   Who scored a record 5 goals for Scotland against Ireland in Belfast in 23 February 1929?
2   In what year was the world record attendance set in the game at Hampden between Scotland and England?
3   The following week, the Scottish Cup final between Celtic and Aberdeen produced an attendance that was only marginally less. Who was the only player who played in both games?
4   Who is the oldest player to have played for Scotland?

5 Who is the youngest player to have played for Scotland?

6 Hampden Park produced an attendance record for a World Cup qualifying tie of 107,580 on 13 October 1965. Who were the opposition that night?

7 Which club has produced the most Internationalists for Scotland?

8 On two occasions Scotland have reached double figures against the same country. Which country?

9 In what year was Scotland's record 3–9 defeat at the hands of England?

10 Who handed out Scotland's biggest World Cup defeat?

11 Who has the dubious honour of being the first Scotsman to be sent off in an International?

12 Who has captained Scotland the most often?

Round

31

Newcastle United

It may seem odd to single out the Magpies (or the Toon Army, as they are sometimes called) for a quiz book on Scotland, but no English team has been so reliant on Scotsmen as Newcastle United have. They are, of course, the closest large English team to Scotland, and have many Scottish supporters. It has long been the author's contention that Newcastle's misfortunes over the last few decades are not unconnected with their modern reluctance to employ as many Scotsmen as they used to!

1 In what year did England play Scotland at St James Park?

2 What was the nickname of Newcastle's great left half of the Edwardian era called Peter McWilliam?

3 From which Scottish team did Hughie Gallacher join Newcastle in 1925?

4 What position did Hughie Gallacher play in the Wembley Wizards game of 1928?

5 In 1929, Hughie scored 5 goals in a game for Scotland.

Who were the opponents?

6   Which ex-Rangers player and Scottish Internationalist was the manager of Newcastle United for a spell in the 1930s?

7   Which Scottish left-winger joined Newcastle United from Third Lanark in 1949 and was nicknamed 'Bobby Dazzler'?

8   How often did Frank Brennan play for Scotland?

9   When Scotland beat England 3–2 in 1967 at Wembley, Scotland's goalkeeper was an ex-Newcastle United man. Who was he?

10   Who was the Scotland captain who also captained Newcastle United to win the Inter Cities Fairs Cup in 1969?

11   Which Scottish Internationalist joined Newcastle United from Celtic in January 1990?

12   Which current member of the Scottish backroom staff played for Newcastle United in two separate spells in the 1970s and the 1990s?

Jock Stein

Jock Stein never played for Scotland, because, as he himself cheerfully admitted, he wasn't good enough. After a very successful managerial career he became their manager in the wake of the Argentina Disaster of 1978. He was always very patriotic, the one face that was instantly recognised on English television screens, and was often regarded as the voice of Scottish football. His achievements are legendary and, frankly, it is unlikely that we will ever 'see his likes again' in the words of a famous song.

1   For which Scottish team, other than Celtic, did Jock Stein play?

2   Which two Scottish teams, other than Celtic, did he manage?

3   Jock was Scotland's manager on a part-time basis in 1965 in an attempt to qualify Scotland for the 1966 World Cup. In what European city were Scotland eliminated from the tournament?

4   He was manager of an English team for a few weeks before he was offered the Scotland job in 1978. Which team?

5   His first game in charge of Scotland was a 3–2 win over Norway at Hampden on 25 October 1978. Who was the captain that night?

6   The game that qualified Scotland for the 1982 World Cup was a rather anticlimactic 0–0 draw in October 1981. Against whom?

7   Arguably, Jock's best result as manager of Scotland was a 3–1 defeat of Spain at Hampden in November 1984. Which three Aberdeen players were in the Scottish team that night?

8   On two occasions in Jock's tenure of the job, Scotland beat England. The score line was the same on both occasions. What was it?

9   In Jock's penultimate game in charge, Scotland were indebted to a man called Jim Bett for a late and rather fortunate winner. Who were the opposition?

10   In what stadium did Jock Stein meet his death?

11   Who was the Chelsea player who played for Scotland that night?

12   Who converted the vital penalty for Scotland that night?

Gordon Strachan

The current Scotland manager is Gordon Strachan. Born in Edinburgh in 1957, there is something very Scottish about this cheery and occasionally cheeky redhead (but the red hair is now sadly disappearing). Although he did not always endear himself to opposition supporters with his antics on the field, he is very definitely a winner, certainly in Scotland. He was a great player, and we all hope that he will become a really great manager.

1   For what Scottish team, other than Aberdeen, did Gordon Strachan play?

2   With Aberdeen, he won many domestic honours and one European success in what used to be called the European Cup Winners Cup. In what year was this?

3   Who did Aberdeen beat in the final of this tournament?

4   Who was his manager at Aberdeen?

5   He then moved on to play in England. Which three English teams did he play for?

6 In what year did he win an FA Cup Winner's medal?

7 In 2005 he became manager of Celtic. He succeeded a man who is now also an international manager. Who was this?

8 His first game as manager of Celtic was an embarrassing 0–5 defeat to a little-known central European team. Who were they?

9 He was manager of Celtic for four seasons. How often did Celtic win the Scottish Premier League in his tenure?

10 Which English team did he then manage after he left Celtic in 2009?

11 He became Scotland's manager in early 2013. His first game was against Estonia. Where was it played?

12 The only goal of the game was scored by a man with connections to both Aberdeen and Celtic. Who was this?

THE ANSWERS

England

1 Surrey.
2 1902 was the Ibrox Disaster. That game was declared unofficial and another game was played at Villa Park, Birmingham.
3 Steve Bloomer.
4 Dixie Dean.
5 Harry Hibbs.
6 Johnny Haynes.
7 Jimmy Greaves.
8 Jimmy Greaves for Roger Hunt.
9 Colin Todd.
10 Terry Butcher.
11 Paul Gascoigne.
12 John Gorman.

World Cup 1954

1 Norway.
2 Helsinki.
3 They were on tour in Canada.
4 Thirteen.
5 Austria.
6 Zurich.
7 Czechoslovakia.
8 Andy Beattie.
9 0–7.
10 Tommy Docherty and Willie Ormond.
11 Basle.
12 West Germany.

Kenny Dalglish

1 102.
2 1977.
3 Pittodrie.
4 Rangers.
5 Luxembourg.
6 Three times.
7 Newcastle United and Blackburn Rovers.
8 Aberdeen.
9 New Zealand.
10 Cumbernauld United.
11 It was a miskick and went through the goalkeeper's legs.
12 30.

The Nineteenth Century

1 Hamilton Crescent, Glasgow.
2 Queen's Park.
3 Racecourse Ground, Wrexham.
4 He scored the first hat-trick for Scotland.
5 They beat England five years in a row.
6 Easter Road, Edinburgh.
7 Wales.
8 Queen Mary.
9 Dundee.
10 It was the first Scottish team to have 'Anglo-Scots' (i.e. Scotsmen who played for English teams).
11 R.S. McColl.
12 Goalkeeper.

Celtic Players

1 Dan Doyle.

2 Jimmy Quinn and Jimmy McMenemy.

3 Paris.

4 7.

5 Bobby Evans, Bobby Collins and Willie Fernie.

6 Pat Crerand.

7 Bobby Lennox.

8 36 years old.

9 Danny McGrain.

10 John Kennedy.

11 Paul McStay.

12 Craig Burley.

World Cup 1958

1 Jackie Mudie.
2 It was on a Sunday and some churches, particularly in the Highlands, objected.
3 West Germany.
4 Switzerland.
5 It was the Manchester United air crash, which seriously injured Matt Busby. No replacement was appointed.
6 Sweden.
7 Tommy Younger.
8 John Hewie.
9 1–1.
10 Paraguay.
11 Notts Forest.
12 Brazil.

Ireland

1 1884.
2 Solitude.
3 11–0.
4 1903.
5 Patsy Gallacher.
6 Hughie Gallacher.
7 Bertie Peacock.
8 Billy Simpson.
9 1961.
10 Ronnie Simpson.
11 Martin O'Neill and Jimmy Nicholl.
12 1984.

Hampden

1 1903.

2 Mount Florida.

3 1906.

4 Willie Reid.

5 1927.

6 The noise caused when Jimmy McGrory scored in 1933.

7 A tenpin bowling alley.

8 The world attendance record of 149,547.

9 November 1954 against Northern Ireland.

10 1970.

11 134,000.

12 Rugby Park, Kilmarnock.

North of the Tay

1 Gordon Smith.
2 Alan Gilzean.
3 Jock Hutton.
4 Everton.
5 The abdication of King Edward VIII.
6 Graham Leggat.
7 Craig Levein.
8 Paul Sturrock.
9 Dundee.
10 Dundee and Aberdeen.
11 Alex McLeish. (He had 77, Miller had 65.)
12 Duncan Shearer.

World Cup 1974

1 Denmark.
2 Jim Holton and Joe Jordan.
3 Willie Ormond.
4 Poland.
5 Northern Ireland.
6 West Germany.
7 Leeds United.
8 John Blackley.
9 Billy Bremner.
10 Yugoslavia.
11 Joe Jordan.
12 West Germany.

Wales

1 9–0.
2 Tynecastle.
3 Billy Meredith.
4 Tannadice.
5 Dublin.
6 It was the first Scotland v. Wales game to be televised live.
7 In the World Cup qualifier of October 1977, played at Anfield.
8 John Hartson.
9 Charles.
10 Hughie Gallacher.
11 Robbie Earnshaw.
12 Willie Donachie.

1 Pittodrie.
2 Lord Rosebery.
3 R.S. McColl.
4 John Campbell.
5 Cappielow.
6 Bobby Templeton.
7 St James' Park, Newcastle.
8 Jimmy Quinn.
9 He was the only man who did not play for, or had not in the past played for, Celtic.
10 McWilliam.
11 1904.
12 Third Lanark.

Denis Law

1 Aberdeen.
2 Huddersfield Town.
3 Wales.
4 The game was abandoned.
5 Torino.
6 Leicester City.
7 Northern Ireland and Norway.
8 1965 and 1967.
9 The European Cup final between Manchester United and Benfica.
10 He returned to Manchester City.
11 Arthur Montford.
12 Zaire.

World Cup 1978

1 Czechoslovakia.
2 Anfield, Liverpool.
3 Third Lanark.
4 Andy Cameron.
5 1–0 for England.
6 Joe Jordan.
7 Don Masson.
8 Willie Johnston.
9 West Bromwich Albion.
10 It was an own goal.
11 Kenny Dalglish.
12 Argentina.

1 Ian McColl.
2 Duncan and Dave MacKay.
3 Second from the left in the front row.
4 Fourth from the right in the back row.
5 Wembley.
6 Jim Baxter.
7 Eddie McCreadie.
8 Tommy Gemmell.
9 1902, before the Ibrox Disaster.
10 There was one! But goalkeepers dressed the same as other players at that time. The clue is the gloves being held by the man (Harry Rennie) in the front row.
11 George Young.
12 Bobby Evans.

Edinburgh Players

1 Willie Bauld.
2 Willie Ormond.
3 Jimmy Dunn.
4 Bobby.
5 John Collins and Darren Jackson.
6 Alec Massie.
7 St Bernard's and Leith Athletic.
8 Jack Harkness.
9 Willie Ormond, Craig Levein and George Burley.
10 Last Minute Reilly.
11 Davie Shaw.
12 Isaac.

1919–1939

1 1927 and 1939.
2 Tommy Cairns.
3 Andy Wilson.
4 Alec Troup.
5 Dave Morris.
6 Hughie Gallacher.
7 Ramsay MacDonald.
8 Bob McPhail to Jimmy McGrory.
9 Jimmy McGrory.
10 Dally.
11 Jimmy Delaney.
12 Bill Shankly.

World Cup 1982

1 Jock Stein.
2 Gordon Strachan.
3 Northern Ireland.
4 The Falklands War.
5 Malaga and Seville.
6 New Zealand.
7 Alan Brazil.
8 Dave Narey.
9 Jimmy Hill.
10 Joe Jordan.
11 Willie Miller and Alan Hansen.
12 Italy.

Wembley

1 1–1.
2 Alex Jackson.
3 Jack Harkness.
4 Alec James.
5 Jimmy Cowan.
6 Dave Mackay, Davie Wilson and Pat Quinn.
7 Jim Baxter.
8 3–2.
9 Denis Law, Bobby Lennox or Jim McCalliog.
10 Stewart Kennedy.
11 The Queen's Silver Jubilee.
12 Don Hutchison.

1946–1980

1 Jimmy Delaney.
2 Henry Morris.
3 Austria.
4 The game was abandoned because of foul play by the Austrians when Scotland were leading 4–1.
5 It was the day after the Aberfan Disaster in Wales.
6 Tommy Gemmell.
7 Bobby Murdoch.
8 The very first International between the two teams in 1872.
9 Brazil.
10 Scotland 0 England 5.
11 Alan Rough.
12 Diego Maradona.

World Cup 1986

1 Mexico.
2 Iceland.
3 Jim Leighton lost one of his contact lenses and had to be replaced by Alan Rough.
4 Davie Cooper.
5 Jock Stein collapsed and died at the final whistle.
6 Australia.
7 Sampdoria.
8 Gordon Strachan.
9 He was sent off in the first few minutes.
10 Richard Gough, Maurice Malpas, Dave Narey, Eamonn Bannon and Paul Sturrock.
11 Jim Leighton.
12 Argentina.

Rangers Players

1 Moses McNeil.
2 Neil Gibson.
3 Alan Morton.
4 Jimmy Simpson.
5 Bobby Brown.
6 Bobby Shearer and Eric Caldow.
7 Davie Wilson, Alec Scott and Ralph Brand.
8 Eric Caldow.
9 Italy.
10 Tam Forsyth.
11 Paul Gascoigne
12 19.

Managers

1 Andy Beattie.
2 Ian McColl.
3 Malky MacDonald.
4 Andy Roxburgh.
5 1965.
6 1–1.
7 Alex Ferguson.
8 Craig Brown.
9 Bertie Vogts.
10 Birmingham City.
11 Bobby and Craig.
12 Tommy Docherty.

World Cup 1990

1 Andy Roxburgh.
2 Italy.
3 Newcastle United.
4 The rich coast.
5 It was scored deep into injury time, added on by the referee because of Cypriot time wasting.
6 Norway.
7 Egypt.
8 Maurice Johnston.
9 Craig Levein and Alex McLeish.
10 Robert Fleck.
11 Brazil.
12 West Germany.

1981–2000

1 Notts Forest.
2 Charlie Nicholas.
3 Canada.
4 Sir Stanley Rous.
5 Richard Gough.
6 Republic of Ireland.
7 He scored the late goal that beat Bulgaria and allowed Ireland to qualify for the 1988 European Championships.
8 Saudi Arabia.
9 Argentina.
10 Portugal.
11 Hiroshima.
12 Germany.

European Championships

1 Sweden.
2 Andy Roxburgh.
3 Richard Gough.
4 Dennis Bergkamp.
5 Andy Goram, Richard Gough or Gordon Durie.
6 The former Soviet Union.
7 Scott Booth.
8 Colombia.
9 Villa Park, Birmingham.
10 Alan Shearer.
11 Ally McCoist.
12 Because they wanted England to score more goals against Holland so that Scotland could qualify on goal difference.

The Twenty-First Century

1 Craig Brown.
2 Joos Valgaeren.
3 Berti Vogts.
4 Faroe Islands.
5 James McFadden.
6 0–6.
7 The Kirin Cup.
8 France.
9 Walter Smith and Alex McLeish.
10 50.
11 Serbia.
12 Croatia.

Anglo-Scots

1 Peter McWilliam.
2 Hughie Gallacher.
3 Bobby Johnstone.
4 Tommy Docherty.
5 Ian St John.
6 Archie Gemmill.
7 Alan Gilzean.
8 Denis Law.
9 Billy Bremner.
10 Bob Wilson.
11 Gary McAllister.
12 Robert Snodgrass.

World Cup 1998

1   Estonia.
2   Monaco.
3   Kevin Gallacher.
4   The funeral of Diana, Princess of Wales was on the 6th.
5   Celtic Park.
6   Brazil.
7   John Collins.
8   Tom Boyd.
9   Tore André Flo.
10 Vidar Riseth.
11 Morocco.
12 Craig Burley.

Records

1 Hughie Gallacher.
2 1937.
3 Jimmy Delaney.
4 David Weir on 3 September 2010, aged 40 years and 116 days.
5 John Lambie on 20 March 1886, aged 17 years and 93 days.
6 Poland.
7 Rangers.
8 Ireland.
9 1961.
10 Uruguay in 1954.
11 Billy Steel in 1951.
12 George Young.

Newcastle United

1   1907.
2   Peter the Great.
3   Airdrie.
4   Centre forward.
5   Ireland.
6   Andy Cunningham.
7   Bobby Mitchell.
8   8 times.
9   Ronnie Simpson.
10 Bobby Moncur.
11 Roy Aitken.
12 Mark McGhee.

Jock Stein

1 Albion Rovers.
2 Dunfermline and Hibs.
3 Naples.
4 Leeds United.
5 Archie Gemmill.
6 Northern Ireland.
7 Jim Leighton, Willie Miller and Alex McLeish.
8 1–0.
9 Iceland.
10 Ninian Park, Cardiff.
11 David Speedie.
12 Davie Cooper.

Gordon Strachan

1 Dundee.
2 1983.
3 Real Madrid.
4 Sir Alex Ferguson.
5 Manchester United, Leeds United and Coventry City.
6 1985.
7 Martin O'Neill.
8 Artmedia Bratislava.
9 Three times.
10 Middlesbrough.
11 Pittodrie.
12 Charlie Mulgrew.

About the Author

David Potter is 66 and lives in Kirkcaldy with his wife Rosemary. He has three children, four grandchildren and a dog. He is a retired teacher of Classics and Spanish, and has written about thirty books on Scottish football and cricket. Other than sport, his interests are drama and the poetry of Robert Burns. His first recollection of watching Scotland was on a flickering minuscule television in the house of a distant relative when he saw Scotland lose 0–7 to Uruguay in the 1954 World Cup, and the experience scarred him for life. Since then he has watched every Scotland game (either in the flesh or on television) or listened to it on the radio.

Also from The History Press

BACK OF THE NET!

ightning Source UK Ltd.
ilton Keynes UK
OW06f1523120615

3415UK00001B/1/P

9 780750 960731